TRY NOT TO LAUGH
CHALLENGE™
JOKE BOOK

AMERICA

Travel Edition

Try Not To Laugh Challenge
BONUS PLAY

Join our Joke Club and get the Bonus Play PDF!

Simply send us an email to:

 TNTLPublishing@gmail.com

and you will get the following:

- 10 Bonus State Jokes
- 10 Hilarious, Never Before Seen Kid Jokes
- An entry in our Monthly Giveaway of a $50 Amazon Gift card!

We draw a new winner each month and will contact you via email!
Good luck! ☺

The Try Not To Laugh ™ Challenge Instructions:

HA
HA

HA
HA

- Face your opponent.

- Take turns reading jokes out loud to each other.

  HINT: Funny faces & noises are fair game!

  HA
  HA

- When someone laughs the other person gains a point.

- Person to get to 3 points is named The Try Not to Laugh CHAMPION!

TRAVEL JOKES

Why do so many people watch videos online during the 4th of July?

Because they're said to be 'so gallantly streaming'!

Why didn't George Washington pick up the phone when freedom called?

He wanted to let freedom ring.

What do you call the President during their Independence Day barbecue?

"The Commander-in-Chef."

Who wrote the fishes' Declaration of Independence?

The Floundering Fathers.

What is good to eat with jam, but explodes when you add fire to it?

Fire-crackers!

Why were the goats jealous about the Independence Day play?

Because it was the rams parts we watched!

Why did the birds throw bananas at the airport?

They were above the fruited planes!

What did the Salt Lake City student say to the teacher?

"Utah-t me well."

What does Uncle Lamb say, on the Sheep's Independence Day?

"I want ewe!"

What do you need when you're having ribs at a 4th of July barbecue?

Stars and wipes forever.

Why can't the Bald Eagle ever go by his first initial?

Because he doesn't want to be a dog (B. Eagle)!

How did the fireworks know they were in love?

Sparks flew!

What is the shorter version of the Declaration of Independence called?

"The Abbreviation of Independence."

What did the Caveman say, when grilling on the 4th of July?

"Hey, fire works!"

What did they tell the Old Flag, when its flag had a baby flag?

"You're a GRAND Old Flag!"

What happened when the vowels were blinded by the fireworks?

O said, "Can U see?"

What was the before and after results of the American Alphabet Makeover?

It went from C to Shining C.

Where does Mickey Mouse look when he's lost his girlfriend?

Minnie-sota!

Who can make sheep super patriotic?

A-Mary-can!

What did the Founding Fathers eat on the first Independence Day cookout?

A Star-Spangled Burger and Freedom Fries!

What's the best dessert you can eat at a 4th of July wedding?

Chapel pie.

What's the most patriotic dog?

A Star-Spaniel Barker.

How did the Founding Fathers call the bald eagle for dinner time?

With the Li-birdy Bell!

What do you call a macaw who is red, white, and blue?

"Parrot-triotic."

How did the Abbreviation Officer
describe Oklahoma?
"Just OK."

During fireworks, what toy is better
to play with than a frisbee?
A BOOM-erang!

What do you call a short movie and
outdoor meal before the fireworks?
A quick flick picnic!

What can you expect during a
4th of July picnic?
The National Ant-them.

What is America's favorite type of music?

The red, white, and Blues.

What did the Founding Fathers say, when they knew the American flag would become famous?

"Keep an eye on that Grand Old Flag!"

Why did the fast hot dog not have any condiments?

They couldn't muster-d up the strength to ketchup.

What's a fisherman's favorite state to get bait?

WORM-mont.

What do you call an eagle who is a lawyer?

'A Legal Eagle.'

How do you know the man really liked his hot dog?

He relished it.

What do they call the location of the Declaration of Independence?

"The Destination of Independence."

What's on the other side of the Bill of Rights?

The Bill of Lefts.

Which superhero loves to eat
tiny hamburgers?

Slider-man.

What's a dog's favorite part of the
4th of July?

The fire-WOOFS!

What is a firework's favorite
hairstyle?

Bangs.

What state isn't in black and white?

COLOR-ado!

What did the Founding Fathers do when they got bored with writing the Declaration of Independence?

They Yankee Doodled!

How do ducks celebrate the 4th of July?

With fire-QUACK-ers!

What's a goat's favorite part of the 4th of July?

The BAA-becue.

Which President was the cleanest?

George Wash-a-ton.

What's a pigeon's favorite part of 4th of July?

The Barbe-COO!

What's another name for the Statue of Liberty's sneeze?

"The Achoo of Liberty."

How did the American flag know it was in trouble?

It got the 'rocket's red glare'!

How did the lightning respond to the firework show?

With shock and awe!

Why are bald eagles bald?
It's hair-editary.

What's between the 'In' and 'dence' on the 4th of July?
Depends.

What's state doesn't like to get phone calls?
TEXT-as.

What newspaper doubles as earrings?
The Boston Lobe.

What city is home to the most worms?

The Big Apple.

What button do astronauts press to stop the fireworks?

"Blast Off."

What was the Declaration of Independence rollercoaster called?

"The Weeeeeeeee the People."

Why can't just 'anyone' live in the White House?

It would be un-presidented!

Which superhero is always asking questions?

Wonder Woman.

Why are fireworks so dramatic?

They do everything with flare.

What did the firecracker say, on the 4th of July?

"I'm having a blast!"

Why were four out of the five Michigan lakes angry?

Because one thought it was Superior!

What does a monument say
when it sneezes?

"Statue!"

Did you hear the police
surrounded Mt. Rushmore?

Yeah, there were several big busts.

What does the midwestern
debtor say?

"Iowa lot of money."

What's a cat's favorite part of the
4th of July?

The PURR-ades.

What state has the most cars?
Rhode Island.

What happened when the tuba fell on the Army man?
"A-flat Major."

What did General Battery say, as he was dying on the battlefield?
"CHARGE!"

Why did the President feel claustrophobic?
He'd been in too many cabinet meetings.

Why did the Steak tell the Chef everything?

Because he was grilling it!

What state is the happiest?

Merry-land!

Why didn't the vulture eat any of his food during the barbecue cookout?

He prefers the leftovers.

What do the White House mailbox and proper nouns have in common?

Capital letters.

MORE FUN AND SILLY JOKES

Why did the cashier get fired?
Nothing seemed to register with him.

What's the hardest liquid to catch?
Running Water.

What did the lamp say to his wife?
"Honey, you're absolutely glowing!"

Why do squirrels take so many risks?
They're used to going out on a limb.

How did the painting get out of jail?
They found out it was framed!

Why didn't the toast go
back to college?
It was burnt out.

Why was the white crayon
self-conscious?
Because he paled in comparison.

What happened to the World
Sugar Association?
It eventually dissolved.

Why can't you trust pants?
They always pocket your money.

What do you call shoes that are undercover?
Sneakers.

How do you know trains are big tattle tails?
They always blow the whistle.

What happened when the wave graduated from high school?
He swelled with pride.

Why couldn't the bird make a decision?

He was always on the fence.

Which color is always greeting people?

"Yellow!"

What do oceans eat?

SAND-wiches.

What is a golfer's favorite kind of bird?

An Eagle.

What did the four sleepy wheels
on the car say?

"We're TIRE-d!"

What did the plumber say, to the
woman who wouldn't stop singing?

"Pipe down!"

What do you get when you cross
fruit with a reptile?

A Banana Snake.

What country never drinks
from a bottle?

Can-A-Da.

What did the teacher bee say to the student bee?

"Bee-have!"

How did the punch go over at the party?

It was a hit!

What did the lid say, when asked about how it was handling the situation?

"Don't worry, I'm on top of it!"

What is a balloons least favorite type of music?

Pop.

What did the coat on the rack say
to the coat on the floor?

"You're off the hook!"

Why are eye shadow, lipstick, and
mascara never mad at each other?

They always make-up!

How much does a lightbulb weigh?

A watt.

What did the pen and pencil
do at the duel?

Draw their weapons.

Why did the Headless Horseman study so much?

He wanted to get a-head!

Why did the butter keep telling jokes?

He was on a roll.

If a King and Queen are a pair when sitting on a throne, what are they when they are sitting on a toilet?

A Royal Flush.

Why can't Monday lift Saturday?

It's a weak day.

Why did the basketball player run away from his breakfast?

Because he was on a fast break.

What did the string say to the scissors, when they were sitting in traffic?

"Don't cut me off!"

Why was the politician out of breath?

He was running for office!

What do you call a lion who works at a mill?

"A Mill-LION-aire!"

Why did the Army Recruiter not understand his Commander's instructions?

He was being too GENERAL.

What is a Gnat's favorite subject in school?

Geogra-flea.

Why did the wife kick the fisherman out of the house?

He was being too crabby.

Why was the Electron always feeling sad?

Because he was so negative.

Why do bats sleep upside down?

They like to hang out.

Why couldn't the arrow make any friends?

It was always pointing at people.

Why did the maid plant trees inside the house?

She was asked to 'spruce it up'!

What happens when you take tea away from a young toad?

He becomes 'oad'.

Why couldn't the lemon just let it go?

He was still bitter about it.

Why did the bird get so mad at the wind?

It really ruffled his feathers.

Why can't you judge a book by its cover?

It's all a front!

Why did the outlet take cold medicine?

He was plugged up.

Why aren't birds allowed to play basketball?

They commit too many fowls!

Why was the baby cow so hyper?

It had too much CALF-eine.

What did the happy proton say to the sad electron?

"Just be positive!"

Why should you always listen to pencils?

They make good points.

How did the cell phone propose?

He gave her a ring!

Why did the solider have trust issues?

He was always on guard.

Who is the best person to sit on?

A Chairman.

What type of tree is part of your hand?

A Palm.

Why do noodles not like being poured out of a pot?

It's such a strain!

Why should you ask a tree for directions?

It will give you a good ROOT!

Why did the gymnast go bankrupt?

She lost her balance.

Why does a grocery store never get in trouble?

It's full of goodies!

Why wouldn't the horse stop talking?

It was stalling.

Why couldn't the broom stay awake?

It was sweepy!

What's the quickest way from A to Z?

Dash in between them!

What did Red say to Purple?

"You've got a bad case of the blues!"

Two astronaunts were preparing
for a trip to Mars.
The first astronaunt said,"Can I bring
my extra luggage on the trip?"
The second astronaunt replied,
"Sure. We've got plenty of space!"

What animal is best at baseball?

A bat.

What did the boss flame say
to his worker?

"You're fired!"

What did the mother owl
say to her funny son?

"You're a hoot!"

What does a writer use to make his bed?

Sheets of paper.

What instrument does a pirate play when he wants people to go away?

A-guitarrrrrrrrgh!

Why wouldn't the owner of a China shop let Curious George in?

She wanted no monkey business!

What shellfish throws balls the best?

A LOB-ster.

What did one say to two when it asked for help?

"You can count on me!"

Why was the wall cold?

It needed another coat.

Why did the toilet paper go to Las Vegas?

It was on a roll.

What sport did the square, circle, and triangle take up?

Figure skating!

Check out our other joke books!

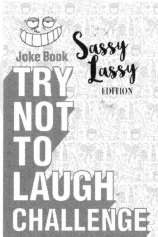

Visit on Amazon Store at:
www.Amazon.com/author/CrazyCorey

Made in the USA
Middletown, DE
30 June 2019